HIDDEN WORLD OF THE
AZTEC

PETER LOURIE

BOYDS MILLS PRESS

HONESDALE, PENNSYLVANIA

For Walker

Additional photographs courtesy of:
INAH, Instituto Nacional de Antropología e Historia: pp. 3, 14, 15, 24 (left), 27, 28 (bottom),
  29 (top & bottom right), 30
Library of Congress: pp. 31, 32, 33
Museo Nacional de Antropología: pp. 12 (painting by Luis Covarrubias), 19 (bottom), 23 (left),
  24 (right, top, and bottom), 43, and cover
Antonio Serrato-Combe: p. 17, Templo Mayor, from *The Aztec Templo Mayor* by Antonio
  Serrato-Combe. Copyright © 2001 by the University of Utah Press. Reproduced courtesy of the
  author and the University of Utah Press
Smithsonian Institution: Icons of Aztec Gods, Victor A. Blenkle Postcard Collection, Archives
  Center, National Museum of American History, Behring Center, Smithsonian Institution: pp. 5, 7,
  13, 17, 21, 27, 31, 35, 37, 41, 45, and cover

Poem fragments from *Fifteen Poets of the Aztec World* by Miguel Leon-Portilla,
  University of Oklahoma Press, 2000. Reprinted by permission.

ACKNOWLEDGMENTS

I would like to thank Leonardo López Luján, Ph.D., director of the Proyecto Templo Mayor and
senior researcher and professor of archaeology at the Museo del Templo Mayor, Instituto Nacional
de Antropología e Historia, for his generous contributions of time and expertise. Special thanks to
Aztec archaeologist Michael E. Smith, Ph.D., Arizona State University, for introducing me to
Leonardo and for checking the facts in the book. My thanks to Saburo Sugiyama, Ph.D., Arizona
State University, who allowed me to explore ongoing excavations in the Moon Pyramid at
Teotihuacan; Laura Filloy Nadal, Ph.D., senior conservator, Museo Nacional de Antropología, INAH,
Mexico City; and to Eduardo Matos Moctezuma, Ph.D., former director of the Museo del Templo
Mayor. Thanks to the students and researchers whose work has enhanced our knowledge of the
Great Temple: Ximena Chávez, Enrico Crucianelli, Minerva Delgado, Agnese Fusaro, Chema García,
Ángel González, Pilar Hernández, Laura Filloy Nadal, Osiris Quezada, Armando Razo, Fabrizio
Sammarco, Federica Taccogna, and Vanessa Tucci.
Lastly, my explorations through the ruins of Mexico's great civilizations would not have been
possible without the assistance of the Instituto Nacional de Antropología e Historia, or INAH.

—P. L.

Library of Congress Cataloging-in-Publication Data

Lourie, Peter.
  Hidden world of the Aztec / by Peter Lourie.— 1st ed.
    p. cm.
  Includes bibliographical references and index.
  ISBN-13: 978-1-59078-069-5 (hardcover : alk. paper)
  1. Templo Mayor (Mexico City, Mexico). 2. Aztecs—Mexico—Mexico
City. 3. Aztec architecture—Mexico—Mexico City. 4. Temples—
Mexico—Mexico City. 5. Excavations (Archaeology)—Mexico—Mexico
City. 6. Mexico City (Mexico)—Antiquities. I. Title.

  F1219.1.M5L68 2006
  972'.01—dc22

                                    2005037353

Boyds Mills Press, Inc.
815 Church Street
Honesdale, Pennsylvania 18431
Printed in China

First edition

10 9 8 7 6 5 4 3 2

Not forever on earth,
only a little while here.
Though it be jade it falls apart,
though it be gold it wears away
        —Nezahualcoyotl,
              fifteenth-century Aztec poet

*T*HE *AZTEC EMPIRE OCCUPIED A HUGE TERRITORY,*
from Central Mexico to the Mexican border with Guatemala, and from the Gulf Coast to the Pacific Ocean. The largest city was the capital, Tenochtitlan, which occupied an island in Lake Texcoco. Earthen roads or causeways linked the city to the mainland. During the fourteenth century, this island was shared by two cities: Tenochtitlan in the south and Tlateloclco in the north. In 1473 Tlatelolco was conquered by the people of Tenochtitlan. The two cities were united, creating a total population of two-hundred thousand inhabitants. Lake Texcoco was drained in the seventeenth century. Tenochtitlan is buried under what is now downtown Mexico City.

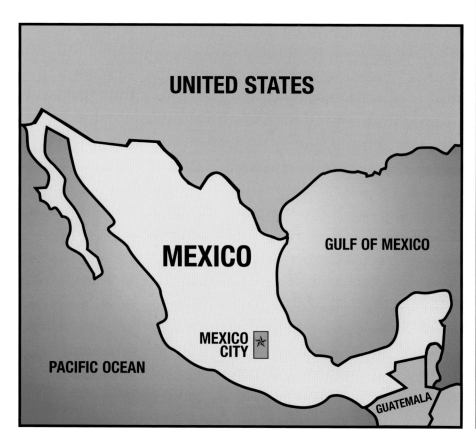

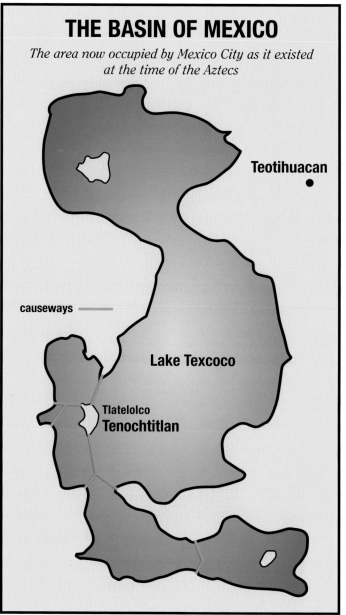

THE BASIN OF MEXICO

The area now occupied by Mexico City as it existed at the time of the Aztecs

Teotihuacan

causeways ———

Lake Texcoco

Tlatelolco
Tenochtitlan

INTRODUCTION

In 1521 the world ended for the Aztec people. A civilization two hundred years in the making came to a sudden and brutal close when the Spanish conquistador Hernán Cortés captured the Aztec capital city of Tenochtitlan (ten-och-tee-TLAHN).

Within months of the conquest, the invaders demolished the Aztec temples, and on top of the rubble, over a flat new surface, a new city emerged. Mansions, churches, and palaces sprung up to form the sixteenth-century beginnings of what is now modern-day Mexico City.

Although the Spaniards tried to erase Aztec culture, Spanish friars and a few conquistadors recorded much about the Aztecs. The Aztecs themselves left a detailed account of their civilization. They wrote poetry, kept records, and documented their rituals and ceremonies. Recent excavations have also greatly contributed to our knowledge of Aztec life.

In order to explore the story of the Aztecs, I followed the well-known archaeologist Leonardo López Luján as he conducted new excavations at both the Aztec Great Temple in downtown Mexico City and the more ancient Pyramid of the Moon in the City of the Gods, just thirty miles north, a place much revered by the Aztecs.

Leonardo's new excavations at the Aztec Great Temple (Templo Mayor in Spanish) were the first diggings here in seven years. And I had the amazing opportunity to be present the week that it all began.

Similarly, the excavation at the more ancient City of the Gods, or Teotihuacan (teo-tee-HUA-can), was the first time archaeologists had ever entered the Pyramid of the Moon from the top. And I got the chance to follow a tunnel deep into the temple to a chamber filled with the skeletons of rattlesnakes, birds of prey, and sacrificial victims.

ONE

THE GREAT TEMPLE

The Zócalo of Mexico City

(left) Excavation at the site of the Great Temple

*In the house of paintings
the singing begins,
song is practiced,
flowers are spread,
the song rejoices.*
—Nezahualcoyotl

My hotel sat on the central plaza of downtown Mexico City, a sprawling metropolis of twenty-five million people. The Plaza de la Constitución, or Zócalo, as it is called, is one of the largest plazas in the world.

From my window, I could see nothing Aztec. But only a few blocks away, the excavation at the Great Temple is a reminder of what lies beneath this city. Once the Spaniards destroyed the Aztec capital, they built their own "colonial" structures. (The colonial period extends from 1521 to 1821, when Mexico declared its independence from Spain.) After 1521, throughout the former Aztec empire, Spanish stone and adobe buildings quickly went up in the cities.

Construction around the Zócalo, where the former Aztec city had had its center, has never stopped. My hotel room looked out at the National Palace, begun by Cortés on the site of Moctezuma II's palace and later remodeled. Its current form dates from 1693. On another side of the Zócalo stands the beautiful Spanish Cathedral, now sitting directly over the ruins of the Aztec Temple of the Sun and other smaller temples. Begun in 1573, this largest of Latin American cathedrals replaced a more modest church that Cortés had built from the materials taken from one of the wrecked pyramids.

Leonardo told me that one of the centuries-old colonial buildings across the street from my hotel was built on top of a famous Aztec palace, the Casas de Axayacatl, named for an Aztec king and father of Moctezuma II. This in fact was the place where Cortés himself was housed as a guest for eight months in 1519 when he first arrived in the Aztec capital.

One story says that while Cortés was there, he ripped down a palace wall to find a room filled with jewelry, head-dresses, textiles, mirrors, fine ceramics, weapons, and many other objects of gold, silver, jade, and obsidian, a smooth jet black volcanic glass. Although he discovered no coins, he found other forms of Aztec money, such as cotton blankets, powdered gold, bronze axes, and cacao beans.

When Leonardo told me this little-known treasure tale, he laughed. He knew I loved treasure stories. He said, "But you're out of luck, Peter. That gold disappeared long ago."

"From this very palace," Leonardo said, "Cortés departed when he went off to conquer the Aztecs in a number of battles before returning finally to storm the Aztec capital."

Leonardo was a perfect guide to lead me through the

Leonardo López Luján

ancient Mexican city of Tenochtitlan. He has been around archaeologists and excavations since he was a little boy. His mother had worked for a famous Maya archaeologist, and when he was growing up, Leonardo and his brother helped wash, mark, and classify ceramic shards. It was difficult work. "If you can do this kind of work and still love archaeology," he said, "then you can do anything in the whole field of archaeology."

A SINKING CITY

I hear a song,
I contemplate a flower . . .
May they never fade!
—Nezahualcoyotl

"Did you know this city is sinking?" Leonardo asked as he led me to the Great Temple through crowded downtown streets.

"Mexico City is built on layers of clay. It used to be a lake, and there is a lot of water in the ground. Always they are pumping water from beneath."

Everything, however, is sinking at different rates. Where modern structures are built on Aztec pyramids, they sink the slowest, so they stay up the highest.

He pointed to the rooftops of the buildings.

Osiris and Enrico at work on the site of the Great Temple

The rise in the rooftops indicates Aztec temples beneath the buildings.

9

"You can see the unevenness of the roof line." Leonardo drew an irregular line with his outstretched hand. "Where the line rises, we know Aztec temples lie beneath the colonial and the modern buildings."

Wherever there is new construction going on, archaeologists try to get there first in order to review the site. He pointed to the back of the cathedral, where there was more construction.

"Five or six years ago, this is where we found the Aztec ball court. And in the chapel we found a beautiful Spanish offering, a small box with gold and silver coins and medals inside, now in the museum.

"Sometimes we are lucky. We might get twenty-eight years for excavations, as we have had at the Great Temple, which is set off from the rest of the city. But other times, sadly, we have very little time before some sort of construction—destruction from an archaeologist's point of view—must begin."

So a lot of the past is lost forever, I thought. Yet I was happy to see Mexico attempting to strike a balance between archaeology and the needs of an ever-expanding modern city.

The Aztec ball court of Tenochtitlan was discovered here behind the cathedral.

AZTEC STONES

Your heart is a book of paintings,
you have come to sing.
—Nezahualcoyotl

When I wasn't with Leonardo at the museum, I watched men in hard hats tear up the street in front of the hotel. There was an ongoing construction project throughout the downtown area. Archaeologists were keeping an eye on the construction because out of the ground the men were bringing up Aztec stones: foundations for the palace that Cortés stayed in and maybe some of the stones from the massive platform that ran around the sacred precinct of the Aztec capital.

In the 1400s, the Aztecs had built glorious temples in this sacred precinct that now covers about fifty acres of Mexico City's historic district, an area equal to about forty-five football fields.

The first excavations of the Great Temple began in the late 1970s at the very center of the Aztec sacred precinct in downtown Mexico City.

TWO

CAPITAL OF THE EMPIRE

*He makes offerings
of flowers and feathers
to the Giver of Life.
He puts the eagle shields
on the arms of the men,
there where the war rages,
in the midst of the plain.*
—Macuilxochitzin,
fifteenth-century Aztec poet

According to their origin myth, the Mexica (me-SHEE-ka) believed they came from Aztlan, a mythical place whose name means "place of white." They left this "place," somwhere in northwestern Mexico, and migrated southward in search of a new home. Archaeologists believe this migration occurred sometime in the twelfth century.

The Mexica, also called Aztec from the word *Aztlan*, were hunters and fishermen. They were familiar with the ways of agriculture. They spoke Nahuatl. Their supreme god was called Huitzilopochtli (hwee-tsee-lo-POSH-tlee), god of war and the sun.

Tenochtitlan: an artist's rendition of the Aztec capital city

A modern "Aztec dancer" on a street in Mexico City

Legend has it that when the Mexica arrived at an island in Lake Texcoco (tesh-KO-ko) in the Basin of Mexico around A.D. 1325, they found the sign that had been foretold to them. Here was the place they were to stop their wandering. It was a place where Aztec myth says an eagle landed on a prickly-pear cactus. The eagle, as legend has it, held a snake in its mouth. So it was here, what is now downtown Mexico City, the Mexica chose to settle.

Using mud and wood at first, the Mexica built the first phase of the Great Temple and founded their capital, Tenochtitlan ("Place of the Hard Prickly Pear"). In the following two centuries, the Great Temple was enlarged twelve times.

Tenochtitlan itself grew in size and sophistication. The Aztecs got most of their food supplies from tribute and commerce. They also created artificial islands in the shallow lake to form foundations for their homes and to grow crops. These *chinampas* were raised fields made of soil that had been placed inside walls of wooden sticks. They were constantly rebuilt by adding new layers of mud and muck (a kind of natural fertilizer) from the bottoms of canals.

Raised-field farming was one of the technological wonders of ancient Mesoamerica. In fact, this was one of

The Mendoza Codex, or book, was created in the sixteenth century by Aztec artists under the supervision of Spanish clerics. The first page, reproduced here, shows an eagle perched on a prickly pear, representing the founding of Tenochtitlan, the Aztec capital city. This image became the symbol on the Mexican flag. In this version, however, there is no serpent in the eagle's mouth. The Mendoza Codex provides a remarkable record of Aztec history, society, and daily life.

the most highly productive preindustrial farming systems anywhere in the world.

As the empire grew, many of its inhabitants, perhaps half of the city's two hundred thousand, went out to farm in the outlying areas beyond the city's center. Over time, the lake disappeared. Today Mexico City sits on top of that old lake bed.

The Aztecs increased their military might. They also established working relations with surrounding peoples. They established governmental and religious hierarchies within their own society, and in the early fifteenth century they worked hard to develop their city. Like the ancient city of Teotihuacan to the north, the Aztec capital was constructed on a grid pattern. The Aztecs built roads and temples and causeways, linking their city to the mainland. An aqueduct system brought water from the mainland.

Various kings, including Moctezuma I, conducted fierce military campaigns and conquered surrounding peoples. A succession of rulers followed until Moctezuma II came to power in 1502, the king Cortés met when he arrived at the city in 1519.

What is remarkable about the Aztecs is that this one group, in less than a hundred years, managed to distinguish itself from the many societies existing at that time. The Aztecs consolidated power and developed a highly structured culture that lasted from the fourteenth to the sixteenth century, when the Spaniards conquered them in 1521.

This ancient Aztec drawing from the Codex Tudela shows various rites dedicated to the God of Death, who sits on a pyramid. At the top left, a priest sacrifices a victim. Below, another priest draws blood from his tongue, and another draws blood from his ear.

THREE

New Excavations at the Great Temple

When they saw that their warriors
fled before them,
the gold sparkling
and the banners of quetzal plumes shining green,
O, do not be taken prisoners!
Let it not be you, make haste!
—Axayacatl,
fifteenth-century Aztec king

The biggest and most important Aztec pyramid was the Great Temple, Huey Teocalli (great temple), also known as Coatepec (Hill of the Serpents) in the Nahuatl language. This temple was built at the very center of the Aztec universe.

I spent mornings with Leonardo and his students on their new excavations on the grounds of the Great Temple.

This digital image by Antonio Serrato-Combe shows what the Great Temple may have looked like.
(left) A serpent's head at the Great Temple

Three pits were being opened up, where Leonardo hoped to find offerings from the first Moctezuma around the time of 1440–1469.

The site of the Great Temple was the place where Aztec myth says the eagle had landed on the cactus, a scene depicted on the modern Mexican flag. Important ceremonies were performed here. The Great Temple was a dual pyramid with a double staircase that led to a single platform. Two shrines at the top were dedicated to the two important Gods of War and Agriculture, Huitzilopochtli and Tlaloc (tla-lok), respectively. Tlaloc was also the God of Rain and the Mountains, where the clouds are born.

The director of the museum, a scholar named Eduardo Matos Moctezuma, who shares the emperor's name (even though there is no relation between the two men, Eduardo likes to joke about this), has written that these two gods symbolize the dual needs of the Aztecs. "Upon these gods depended the dualities of daily subsistence: water and warfare, agricultural production and imperial tribute, hymn to life and hymn to death. . . ."

AZTEC WRITING

With flowers You paint,
O Giver of Life!
With songs You give color,
with songs You shade
those who will live on earth . . .
—Nezahualcoyotl

Laura and Pilar examine a find.

Writing and reading were specialized skills in Aztec society. Most Aztec people were illiterate and had no need for writing in their daily lives. Scribes came from families of former scribes, and each scribe had specific jobs. Some recorded the lineage of the rulers, lords, and noblemen. Some, like geographers, painted the boundaries of cities and villages. Some scribes kept the law books and some others recorded the details of rites and ceremonies.

Only a few preconquest texts, or codices, survived. Each codex, as one of these "books" is called, is a long strip of paper up to thirteen yards long. Aztec paper was made from cloth, deerskin, or the bark of certain fig trees and was folded like a modern map.

The Aztec Calendar, or Sun Stone, was carved in the fifteenth century. It is nearly twelve feet in diameter and three feet thick, and weighs close to twenty-five tons. The calendar, discovered in 1790 beneath the Zócalo, or main plaza of Mexico City, illustrates the Aztecs' knowledge of astronomy and mathematics.

The Aztecs wrote by painting symbols, or glyphs. These symbols conveyed an idea as a picture. The idea of death, for example, might be represented by a corpse wrapped for burial. The idea of walking might be pictured as a trail of footprints. The Aztecs also used color in their glyphs, which added meaning to the pictures.

The Aztec numbering system was based on groups of 20. And as with the Maya, the Aztec maintained two parallel calendars. One was the solar or agricultural calendar, in which the year was divided into 365 days (18 months of 20 days each, plus 5 days). The other calendar was the 260-day ritual calendar, used only by priests to divine the future.

An Aztec "book," or codex

FOUR

THE PROCESS OF ARCHAEOLOGY

Now put on
the necklaces of flowers.
Our flowers from the season of rain. . . .
—Nezahualcoyotl

Leonardo explained the process of excavating. One of the most important and also time-consuming tasks of all, he said, is drawing and measuring. Archaeologists constantly draw as they dig. First they outline the working area with chalk and string. Then everything is drawn—each stone, each slab— one by one, in order to record the distribution of the stones, on the plaza floor in this case, before the digging begins. Leonardo and his students also take digital photographs and videos during this initial phase of excavation and all through the diggings. "Then we take the stone slabs up to begin the excavation of the pit."

Little by little the archaeologists began digging with trowels and brushes, slowly moving down through the dirt.

I followed Leonardo as he moved from pit to pit to check the ongoing work of his students. As he was taking a digital video of this early work, he said, "It's difficult to say for sure what we'll find here, but we have pretty good ideas based on other offerings we've found at the Great

(right) Ángel records the location of each stone.
(left) Chema and Osiris carefully sift through layer upon layer of earth.

Hammers and chisels: tools of the archaeologist's trade
(left) Ángel, Fabrizio, and Federica remove stone after stone.

Temple over almost three decades. In 1980, for instance, we found, right there between those two serpent heads, a stone box containing thirteen images of the rain god Tlaloc, all made of jade. We are excavating these pits not only to discover remains of offerings and burials but also to understand how the pyramid was built."

Leonardo said it's always exciting to begin an excavation because you never know exactly what will turn up. But what made these new pits particularly exciting, he said, was the process of excavation. From years of experience, he and his colleagues had become much better at it. Sometimes how you excavate is as important as what you find. In the old days important information was lost in some of the digging because it was poorly done.

Made from a human skull, this mask represents the God of Death. The eyes are made of shell and pyrite. Sacrificial knives, symbols believed to represent the cutting off of air, are inserted in its nasal cavity and mouth. The small holes in the top of the skull were probably used to attach either human hair or some other material that looked like hair.

BLOOD AND SACRIFICE

*It is not certain that we live
and have come on earth to be happy.
We are all sorely lacking.
Is there any who does not suffer
here, besides the people?*
—Nezahualcoyotl

It might seem strange to us that the Aztecs took lives in order to ensure that life would continue. Aztec rituals of bleeding and sacrifice of warriors horrified the Spaniards when they first arrived. Perhaps none of us today can really imagine what it was like to be Aztec. Religion ruled the common person's life. In an Aztec's adobe-and-thatch hut there most always was a shrine.

Blood was considered to be "most precious water." At the Great Temple warriors were sacrificed on altars, their hearts ripped from their living bodies. The blood nurtured the cult images of the Sun and the Earth and then ran down the temple walls. Sacrifice ensured that life would follow death.

The logic ran something like this: The most precious thing we possess is our blood and, of course, our hearts. Human beings are in debt to the gods because the gods created them and because the gods give them food—animals and vegetables. So, in order to pay these debts, human beings periodically have to offer their own blood (self-sacrifice) as well as the blood of sacrificial victims (women, children, men, warriors, etc.). In this way, the gods are

The Aztec heart extraction ritual is depicted here in the sixteenth-century Codex Magliabechiano. The Aztecs honored their gods with human sacrifice. By offering the most precious thing in life, namely blood, they hoped that new life would spring from death.

Sacrificial knife

nourished: the Sun can continue its daily cycle, and the Earth goddess can give crops to the people.

As with the Maya before them, Aztecs believed that sacrifice also mirrored the cycle of nature. The dry season, the season of harvesting, is followed by rains that again fertilize the soil. So, too, the sacrificing of humans ensured that the human cycle would continue. In fact, there could well be dire consequences if that blood stopped flowing. At least, that's how the Aztecs might have perceived it—very important stuff if you think your whole society, your family, your universe depends on rain and cycles of nature. Many of us modern types have lost our connection to that cycle, which makes it even more difficult to comprehend what the Aztecs were doing.

The Spaniards wrote that thousands of people were sacrificed at the Great Temple in a single day. Archaeologists don't believe this figure. There is no evidence of mass sacrifice at the Great Temple.

The conquering Spaniards exaggerated the numbers. On the other hand, some people in Mexico today want to believe there were no Aztec sacrifices, none at all, that they were merely a fabrication of the Spaniards to justify their conquest. Leonardo does not believe there were none. But there were far fewer human sacrifices than the Spaniards reported. From thirty years of excavations at the Templo Mayor, Leonardo has evidence of only fifty to fifty-five decapitated heads, not thousands. He thinks far too much has been made of Aztec sacrifices.

"We do have a few skeletons of children, too," said Leonardo who had excavated a part of the temple where forty-two skeletons of children were discovered. The children, from six to eight years old, were sacrificed to Tlaloc, the God of Rain, because the Aztecs thought that if a child cries during the sacrifice (his tears being wet like rain), then the rainy season was assured and food would be plentiful for the people. When I mentioned to Leonardo that kids liked to read about the Aztecs in particular because of the blood and sacrifice, he said again, and forcefully, that too much had been made of this part of Aztec culture.

As Leonardo talked, I kept thinking how difficult it is to balance one aspect of a culture with another. How, for example, could I accept the Aztec concepts of death and sacrifice, which frightened me and seemed so alien, with their beautiful sense of architecture and civic design?

THE AZTEC UNIVERSE

If it should happen thus, we will cry like eagles,
we will roar like tigers,
we the old eagle warriors.
—Axayacatl

The Aztec universe was complex. As with other pre-Hispanic peoples in Mexico, their cosmos was divided into three parts: the world above (heavens), the terrestrial world (earth), and the world below (underworld). The heavens had thirteen levels; the underworld had nine. The heavens were separated from the earth and the underworld by five large trees, one at the very center of the cosmos and four at the cardinal points—north, south, east, and west.

In the first four heavens could be found the Sun, the Moon, the Rain, the Clouds, the Comets, the Wind, and the Stars. Then came nine upper heavens where the gods lived. All thirteen heavens were related to the male, the eagle, dryness, light, and the Sun. In the thirteenth level lived Ometeotl (o-me-TEO-tl), God of Duality, representing the two gods who created the world.

Underneath the earth was Mictlan with nine levels. The underworld was very cold, completely dark, and really stinky. It was a place of decomposition, a place where the powers of fertility were generated. The nine levels of the underworld were related to the female, the jaguar, humidity, and obscurity. In the ninth level of the underworld lived Mictlantecuhtli (MICT-lan-tay-KOOT-lee) and Mictecacihuatl (meek-tay-kah-SEE-wahtl), the God and Goddess of Death.

FIVE
GOD OF DEATH

Think on this, O lords,
eagles and tigers,
though you be of jade,
though you be of gold,
you also will go there,
to the place of the fleshless.
We will have to disappear,
no one can remain.
—Nezahualcoyotl

At lunch break Leonardo took me into the basement of the Great Temple Museum, where conservators were working on various projects. Archaeologist Ximena Chávez was piecing together a sacrificed child's bones from the sixteenth century. These bones were found in the 1980s. Thirty years later, someone was now working on the remains. I could see that nothing in archaeology happens fast.

Leonardo pulled a plastic covering off a statue he discovered years ago. I reeled back with a start because it was a monstrous and grotesque figure with a large head

(left) Leonardo and the God of Death

The God of Death buried below a Mexico City street

When discovered, this statue was in a thousand pieces.

Ximena pieces together sixteenth-century bones.

It took Armando long hours of work to uncover the statue.

and exaggerated features, especially its liver that dangled in its hollow chest cavity.

"Here is the God of Death, Mictlantecuhtli. In 1994 we dug several tunnels in the House of the Eagles, where I found this statue. A friend of mine restored it," Leonardo told me. "It took years. Can you imagine the work! When we found it, it was in a thousand pieces. Now this statue is going to an exhibit in London.

"You can see that it is a depiction of the body in the midst of decomposition, not just a skeleton. Notice the ears and the liver," said Leonardo.

Leonardo went on to explain that the liver was enlarged because it was the organ that represented death. The Aztecs believed that a person had three souls: the soul

A photograph documents the date of the excavation of the statue's torso.

Minerva measures an Aztec vase.

of the head, which is related to the nine upper heavens; the soul of the heart, related to the Sun, the first four heavens, and the earth's surface; and the soul of the liver, which is related to the underworld. The God of Death, he said, is always represented with a huge liver.

"And look here." Leonardo pointed at the skull. Plugs of hair protruded from the statue's scalp.

"Wow," I said. "Is that real?"

"Yes, it's real because the God of Death is always represented with curly hair."

It was a frightening sight. I could imagine how lifelike this statue of death would have appeared to the Aztecs with its human hair.

Digging revealed the face of the God of Death

A battle between Spaniards and Aztecs

SIX

THE CONQUEST

Again and again afflicted,
the Mexica exert themselves.
My grandchildren, those of the painted faces,
from the four sides they sound their drums
the flower of the shields remains in your hands.
—Axayacatl

In 1519 Hernán Cortés and a small army of Spanish conquistadors marched into Tenochtitlan, the Aztec capital city built in the middle of beautiful Lake Texcoco. Waiting for the Spaniards was Moctezuma II, the ninth emperor of the royal house established during the second half of the fourteenth century. Moctezuma was a semidivine figure; his subjects never looked directly into his eyes when they spoke.

The Aztec ruler had first heard of the arrival of the Spaniards months before, when he received a folded text from a merchant in the Yucatán that depicted three white temples at sea floating on large canoes. The king had hoped Cortés would bypass the capital. He had been greatly worried of late, especially since at this time there had been a series of bad omens in the city. Strange comets appeared

Moctezuma II

Hernán Cortés

in the sky. The thatch roof on Huitzilopochtli's chapel at the top of the Great Temple burned uncontrollably. Fishermen brought the emperor a rare ashen-colored, cranelike bird. Legend has it that a mirror appeared on the bird's head, and in that mirror the emperor saw men riding on deer dressed for war. Like all Aztecs, Moctezuma believed in omens and symbols.

To keep the Spaniards out of the city, the king sent them gifts. But his messengers returned to say that the strangers, with faces of chalk and clothed for war, were coming to Tenochtitlan no matter what. Moctezuma wept openly, and his extreme distress was felt by his people.

So why did Moctezuma let the strangers keep coming toward his city? Why didn't he wipe them out with his

powerful army? One explanation is that he thought they were gods. Gods to the Mexica were not saints. Gods often behaved badly; they were flawed like humans. So the reports that the Spaniards were humanlike would not have prevented the Aztecs from thinking they might be gods, and one does not attack gods.

Moctezuma's probable conclusion was that Cortés was a lord returning to reclaim his land. Cortés said later that he was welcomed like "a lost leader." Another explanation is that the emperor may have thought Cortés was the reincarnation of the much-revered half-god, half-human Feathered Serpent, Quetzalcoatl (ket-sal-KO-atl).

CAPTURE

Desperate, Moctezuma tried everything. He sent presents of gold and silver and elaborate foods, including turkeys and tortillas sprinkled with the blood of sacrificial victims. Cortés and his men were horrified by the blood. Moctezuma even sent wizards and magicians, perhaps with the hope they could put spells on the strangers.

Cortés and his army continued marching, and on the Aztec day of 1 Wind, they entered Tenochtitlan. Coincidentally, 1 Wind is Quetzalcoatl's Day, attributed to the whirlwind, when robbers and wizards do their mischief.

Once in the city, Cortés and his men were treated magnificently, as was the Aztec custom. Moctezuma, however, wanted to know what it would take for the Spaniards to leave. Cortés replied, "We Spanish suffer from a disease of the heart, which can be cured only by gold."

Cortés then took Moctezuma hostage, falsely claiming

The Spaniards' first view of the Aztec capital

The meeting between Cortés and Moctezuma

The capture of Moctezuma

The battle for the city

that the emperor had ordered an attack on his forces on the coast. A bloody battle raged between the Aztecs and Spaniards. Cortés fought his way to the Great Temple, ascended with the captive king, and tried to negotiate with Moctezuma's people.

Moctezuma died soon afterward. Cortés said he was killed by a stone. Others said he was strangled by the Spaniards and thrown from a rooftop. The Spaniards then had to fight their way out of the city.

During the ensuing campaign against the Aztecs, Cortés recruited many Indian allies who had been enemies of Moctezuma. Meanwhile, a smallpox epidemic, brought by the Europeans, devastated the Aztec population.

The last battle for the Aztec empire took place in 1521. Cortés surrounded the capital and cut off its supply of food and water. The Aztecs sacrificed Spanish soldiers and rolled their heads along the causeways in the lake. The lake was said to have turned red with blood. The final battle raged for three months until Cortés and his men reached the sacred precinct of Tenochtitlan, and the fight was over at last.

SEVEN

DISCOVERY

Grasp your flowers and your fan.
With them go out to dance!
—Nezahualcoyotl

One morning at the Great Temple, I arrived to discover there had been a new find. Leonardo told me how a monolith had been discovered in the corner of a nearby colonial building that was being renovated. Leonardo said, "This Aztec monolith was used in colonial times to decorate the corner of the building. It was exposed to pedestrians in the eighteenth and nineteenth centuries. But sometime in the nineteenth century, the level of the street was elevated and the monolith was covered up. Nobody remembered it was there."

Based on a 1794 drawing that Leonardo had studied while in Paris the previous year, he knew that this monolith might be somewhere near the corner of the building under the sidewalk. He thought it would take a while to find it, but on the previous day when they pulled a manhole cover from the sidewalk of a busy street, by chance there it was, just one meter under the surface surrounded by electrical wires.

"It was described in the eighteenth century as being a claw, but in fact it is a barrel cactus, and you can see here. . . ." He held out a digital photo taken the day before. "Look at the blue paint from the flowers on the stucco." Leonardo was excited.

Armando and Chema excavating the Aztec monolith, a major engineering feat

The monolith was Aztec and the style, he said, showed that it was made at the end of the fifteenth century or the beginning of the sixteenth.

"I think this monolith of ours is a very important discovery. What we are going to do is excavate inside the building to make a small tunnel and then pull it from the corner. Maybe in about one month we'll have this monolith inside the museum. Do you want to see it?"

"Absolutely," I said. I couldn't wait.

An assistant pulled up the manhole cover. I dropped my head into the quiet, dank darkness. I pointed a flashlight to a far wall, and then I saw it. Incredible. A small fraction of the large stone peered out of the rubble. Beneath the busy street was a silent, ancient space where this monolith had sat for centuries—a veritable treasure under the feet of unsuspecting thousands.

(left) Chema looks below the busy street at the Aztec monolith.

EIGHT

PYRAMID OF THE MOON

O my lords!
Thus we are,
we are mortal,
humans through and through.
—Nezahualcoyotl

Leonardo felt it was important for me to spend at least one full day at the older city of Teotihuacan, a place that the Aztecs had called the City of the Gods. Teotihuacan, which flourished from about A.D. 300 to 900, was the center of an ancient civilization that preceded the Aztecs. When the Aztecs saw the ruins of the city, they thought gods had lived there. Only gods could build structures so big.

The city plan and the pyramids at Teotihuacan were models that the Aztecs used when constructing their own capital city of Tenochtitlan.

Leonardo had been helping another archaeologist from Japan in an exciting excavation at the Pyramid of the Moon. Saburo Sugiyama was excavating in the fourth and fifth phases of the huge temple. He had identified seven phases in its three-hundred-year construction. Saburo

(left) The Pyramid of the Moon   *Dr. Saburo Sugiyama*   37

Avenue of the Dead, with the Pyramid of the Sun in the background

had worked all summer long taking dirt out, and now things were being discovered every day.

Teotihuacan, contemporary with Rome and the classic city-states of the Maya, was the largest New World civilization of its time. At the height of its prosperity in the year A.D. 400, Teotihuacan had as many as 125,000 inhabitants and was the sixth-largest city in the world.

For centuries Teotihuacan was a sophisticated urban center before its collapse in the seventh century A.D. Although we don't know for sure what toppled the city, many believe its demise came from within its own society. The civic order may have broken down until a conscious decision was made to destroy the city. Palaces were burned and temples were reduced to rubble.

The name for the city Teotihuacan is a Nahuatl word.

We do not even know what it was called by its own people, nor do we have a record of the language they spoke.

Although it had long ago disappeared by the time the Great Temple was built, we know that it was a sacred place to the Aztecs. Much of Aztec architecture, cosmology, religion, art, and thought was derived from Teotihuacan, a city that had its heyday a thousand years before the rise of the Aztecs.

The amazing thing, Leonardo told me, is that there are so many unanswered questions at this ancient city. Archaeologists have been unable to decipher the writing, and much of the history of the city is not known, either. Big questions still exist about the social and religious organization of its society. No royal tombs had yet been located at Teotihuacan. Leonardo hoped to find one some day.

Early one morning Leonardo drove me out of the city,

Excavating at the site of one of the many temples

through a sprawl of cars and polluted air. A few hours later we were walking up the Avenue of the Dead, which runs through the center of Teotihuacan. We stopped at the terminus of this five-kilometer main city axis and stood at the base of the massive Pyramid of the Moon. Here was an intact temple of identical size to the Great Temple back in Mexico City.

"You ready? Let's go," said Leonardo as he began to climb the outside wall of the temple. Straight up!

"But what about the stairs?" I said. Although steep, the stairs that ran up the center of the pyramid looked like the safest way to ascend.

"It's faster this way," he said.

I followed, gasping for air when we reached the tunnel entrance near the top.

Before entering, however, I turned to look at the ruins of the city. How beautiful it was! Just as in the Aztec capital, the streets were laid out in an obvious grid pattern. Other pyramids lined the Avenue of the Dead. The largest temple, the Pyramid of the Sun, faced west and stood at the center of the northern section. To get a perspective on the temple's size, Leonardo told me the Pyramid of the Sun has the same horizontal dimensions at its base as the Great Pyramid of Giza, but it is not as high (the Sun Pyramid is only 67 meters high; the Egyptian pyramid is 145 meters).

Here, too, was the temple of the Feathered Serpent (Quetzalcoatl), such an important god in Mesoamerican cultures. So many other temples yet to be excavated were simply mounds of dirt and grass. In fact, I learned that only 5 percent of Teotihuacan had been excavated so far.

I turned to enter the tunnel.

Sifting through material dug from the Pyramid of the Moon

NINE

INTO THE HEART OF THE PYRAMID

*I look into their faces,
eagles and tigers on all sides;
from experience I recognize the jade
the precious bracelets. . . .*
—Nezahualcoyotl

I felt like Indiana Jones as I inched my way through the narrow tunnel. I could hear a loud hum from an electric generator that powered the bare bulbs strung intermittently along the dark shaft. Using a ladder, I dropped through a hole in the floor and then through another tunnel.

Suddenly I came into a dimly lit room where Leonardo joined two other archaeologists who were scraping at artifacts in a small rectangular pit. The ceiling of the space was low, and the air was dusty. Steel girders ran the length of the cavity to keep the room from caving in.

Saburo was at the center of the pit, examining some jade beads the size of birds' eggs. At the far end of the room, two men were piling dirt into buckets to take outside, and I had to move with difficulty to get out of their way. The backfill would be sifted for artifacts and the soil tested for plant life.

(left) Leonardo enters the heart of the pyramid.

A worker greets us in the dark tunnel.

Saburo at work deep in the pyramid

Archaeologists found evidence that many warriors were buried here.

Balanced on the steel girders, I shifted around, taking photos. Leonardo was down in the dirt with Gregory Pereira, a French archaeologist, discussing today's finds. They had been working on two skulls, probably warriors. They brushed off dirt so they could take photographs before removing them. In the past few days they had found, among other treasures, jade beads and some huge seashells. They also had found figurines made from obsidian. Among the skulls and jade objects were the skeletons of rattlesnakes.

Because so many warriors were buried here, the archaeologists were finding many projectile points, too. Today, they had even found the skull of a puma. All of these objects would be photographed and videotaped, then drawn, then carefully lifted out two or three days from now.

At that point the archaeologists would move down to the next layer.

In order not to get in anyone's way, I left fairly soon. While Leonardo worked the rest of the day, I explored the city and met him later for the ride back to my hotel. In the car, Leonardo mentioned that some experts believe there are no royal tombs at the ancient city because this society had a completely different kind of social organization than the Maya, for instance. "But we think they did bury their rulers in great tombs somewhere in the city, perhaps even in the Pyramid of the Sun itself."

Leonardo told me that when Saburo's excavations were finished, everything would be backfilled to help prevent looters from coming in. The backfill would contain large rocks, which would make digging very difficult.

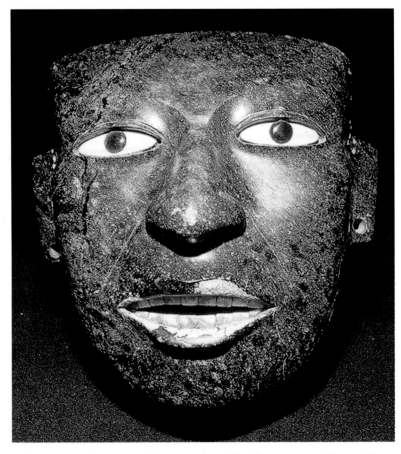

The Aztecs discovered this mask at Teotihuacan and brought it back to the Great Temple.

Teotihuacan offered sacrifices, and we think this may have been the model for Aztec sacrifice."

I was impressed by the idea that one great culture assimilates so much from another great culture. In fact, the Aztecs came frequently to Teotihuacan to excavate for objects that they then brought back to the Great Temple. These objects became part of Aztec ceremony. And Aztec priests may well have performed their own rituals in front of the abandoned pyramids of the older culture.

It had been a magical day, full of quiet and mystery, but now the loud city was upon us.

> *Not forever on earth,*
> *only a little while here.*
> —Nezahualcoyotl

As we entered the traffic of one of the biggest cities in the world, Leonardo said, "There is a sixteenth-century source that relates how the Aztec king Moctezuma used to come every twenty days to the ruins at Teotihuacan to give presents to the gods. We have evidence that the people of

 # EPILOGUE

We all will have to go away,
we all will have to die on earth . . .
Like a painting
we will be erased.
Like a flower,
we will dry up
here on earth.
—Nezahualcoyotl

I said good-bye to Leonardo with a hearty handshake and turned toward my hotel on the Zócalo. Tomorrow I was leaving, but of course I knew I'd return to Mexico. So much more was waiting to be explored.

Construction outside the hotel had stopped for the night. Aztec stones lay on the pavement. Cars buzzed past the National Palace and rounded the sixteenth-century cathedral like frantic insects.

Beneath Mexico City, the temples of another great city slumbered. Through five hundred years of sleep, those Aztec temples were very much alive.

(left) A dragon carved from stone at Teotihuacan

Aztec wonders lie hidden beneath the streets of Mexico City.

GLOSSARY

Axayacatl: sixth ruler of the Aztec people, 1469–1481. He took power after the rule of Moctezuma I.

Aztec: *Azteca* means "someone who comes from Aztlan," a mythical place in Mexico. The term *Aztec* describes the culture that dominated the Basin of Mexico in the fifteenth and sixteenth centuries.

Aztlan: a mythical place in Mexico. The Aztecs claimed they came from Aztlan when they settled on an island in a big lake, on which Mexico City now stands.

chinampas: raised fields made of soil, rebuilt continually by the Aztecs in order to build homes and grow highly productive crops in Lakes Texcoco, Xochimilco, and Chalco.

codex (singular), codices (pl): Aztec sacred books and other native books made of bark paper, deerskin, or cloth (during the colonial period); known in Western scholarship as codices.

colonial period: a time period in Mexico's history that began from the conquest in 1521 to 1821, when Mexico declared its independence from Spain.

Cortés, Hernán: (1485–December 2, 1547); the conquistador who conquered Mexico for Spain.

Feathered Serpent, Quetzalcoatl: Creator God that represented the duality of nature. Half air and half earth, the feathered serpent was one of the most important pre-Hispanic deities.

Huitzilopochtli: patron god of the Aztecs, meaning "Left-Handed Hummingbird." Hummingbirds and eagles are very aggressive birds, and the Aztecs related them to war. Huitzilopochtli was also the Sun God, whom the Aztecs fed with human sacrifice.

jade: a strong, typically green gemstone that takes on a high polish; used for jewelry, ornaments, and sculpture. To the Aztecs jade was associated with precious things, beings, and water. Jade was even more important than gold.

Lake Texcoco: a former lake in central Mexico. Texcoco has been drained since the early seventeenth century. Tenochtitlan, the Aztec capital, captured in 1521 by the Spanish conquistador Hernán Cortés, stood on islands in old Texcoco, connected to the mainland by causeways. In fact, there were five lakes: Chalco and Xochimilco to the south, Texcoco in the center, and Xaltocán and Zumpano to the north.

Mesoamerica: refers to a region of Central America and southern North America (including the present-day countries of Mexico, Guatemala, Belize, Honduras, and El Salvador) that was occupied by several civilizations.

Mexica: another name for the Aztecs, the inhabitants and founders of Tenochtitlan and Tlatelolco. *Mexica* means "the people of Mexi." Mexi, according to most scholars, is another name for Huitzilopochtli. The Mexicas were ethnically Nahuas and spoke Nahuatl, the common language at that time. The

Aztecs, during their migration, found an eagle (Huitzilopochtli), which told them that they would no longer be called *Mexicas*, but rather *Aztecs*. So they changed their name.

Mexico City: capital city of Mexico located in a large basin on a high plateau, surrounded on many sides by volcanoes more than 16,000 feet high.

Mictecacihuatl: Goddess of Death; ruled Mictlan with Mictlantecuhtli.

Mictlan: the Aztec underworld, ruled over by its God and Goddess. It was a gloomy place, completely dark, very cold, and stinky. It was reached by the dead only after wandering for four years beneath the earth, accompanied by a "soul-companion," a dog, which was customarily cremated with the corpse.

Mictlantecuhtli: God of Death, ruler of Mictlan.

Moctezuma I: ruler of the Aztecs from 1440 to 1469.

Moctezuma II: ruler of the Aztecs who governed Tenochtitlan between the years 1502 and 1520 with relative peace, until the Spaniards arrived.

Nahuatl: the language of the Aztec people (and many other peoples from central Mexico). Nahuatl, the main native language in present-day Mexico, is spoken by 1.5 million people today.

obsidian: natural glass of volcanic origin, typically jet black in color.

Quetzalcoatl: see *Feathered Serpent*

Tenochtitlan: ancient city in the central basin of Mexico. Founded around A.D. 1325 on a marshy island in Lake Texcoco, the city covered an area of 13.5 square kilometers and had as many as 200,000 inhabitants.

Teotihuacan: a religious center in the Mexican Highlands around the time of Christ. From A.D. 1 to 200, monumental construction began, during which Teotihuacan quickly became the largest and most populous urban center in the New World. (It was actually the sixth-biggest city in the whole world.) The city appears to have expanded to approximately 20 square kilometers, with about 100,000 inhabitants. It was burned around A.D. 600.

Tlaloc: the Aztec Rain God. He is pictured as a man wearing a net of clouds, a crown of heron feathers, and foam sandals and carrying rattles to make thunder. Tlaloc's name means "He Who Makes Things Sprout." Greatly feared, the god could provoke drought and hunger or hurl lightning on the earth. Tlaloc also had goggled eyes and fangs.

Zócalo: the central plaza of downtown Mexico City, also called the Plaza de la Constitución.

INDEX

BIBLIOGRAPHY

Baquedano, Elizabeth. *Eyewitness Books: Aztec, Inca and Maya*. New York: Alfred Knopf, 1993.

Boone, Elizabeth H. *The Aztec World*. Washington, DC: Smithsonian Institution Press, 1996.

Defrates, Joanna. *What Do We Know About the Aztecs?* New York: Peter Bedrick Books, 1992.

López Luján, Leonardo. *The Offerings of the Templo Mayor of Tenochtitlan*. Translated by Bernard R. Ortiz de Montellano and Thelma Ortiz de Montellano. Boulder: University Press of Colorado, 1994.

López Luján, Leonardo, and Judy Levin. *Tenochtitlan*. New York: Oxford University Press. 2005.

Matos Moctezuma, Eduardo. *The Great Temple of the Aztecs*. New York: Thames and Hudson, 1988.

Smith, Michael E. *The Aztecs*, 2nd edition. Malden, MA: Blackwell Publishers, 2003.

Soustelle, Jacques. *Daily Life of the Aztecs on the Eve of the Spanish Conquest*. Stanford: Stanford University Press, 1961.

Steele, Philip. *The Aztec News: The Greatest Newspaper in Civilization*. Cambridge, MA: Candlewick Press, 1997.

Townsend, Richard F. *The Aztecs*, revised 2nd edition. New York: Thames and Hudson, 2000.

Whittington, E. Michael, editor. *The Sport of Life and Death: The Mesoamerican Ballgame*. Charlotte, NC: Thames and Hudson, 2001.

Wood, Tim. *The Aztecs (See-Through History)*. New York: Viking Books, 1992.

WEB SITES

The following sites were active at the time of publication.

Author's Web site: peterlourie.com

Aztec Links (links to information about Aztec calendars, jewelry, history, religion, economy, society, writings, and much more).
http://www.mysteries-megasite.com/main/bigsearch/aztec.html

Foundation for the Advancement of Mesoamerican Studies Inc.
http://www.famsi.org/

Museum of the Great Temple, Mexico City.
http://archaeology.la.asu.edu/tm/index2.php

Teotihuacan: The City of the Gods. Saburo Sugiyama's Teotihuacan home page at Arizona State University; a great resource to explore this ancient city.
http://archaeology.la.asu.edu/teo/